Sorting

Karina Law

W

FRANKLIN WATTS
LONDON·SYDNEY

Contents

Sorting shapes   **4**

Wash day   **6**

Tidy up time!   **8**

Lots and few   **10**

Sorting materials   **12**

Dinner time!   **16**

Fair sorting   **18**

Sorting shopping   **20**

Make a sorting box   **22**

Word picture bank   **24**

Look out for Tiger on the pages of this book. Sometimes he is hiding!

Every day we sort things in different ways.

food

paper

cars

coins

jigsaw pieces

3

Sorting shapes

We sort things into groups.

I am sorting different shapes.

Round

Straight

Wash day

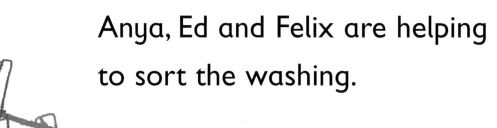

Anya, Ed and Felix are helping
to sort the washing.

6

We sort the dry clothes and put them away. They will be easy to find.

I am sorting these socks into pairs. Can you find an odd sock?

Tidy up time!

Mum asks Harrison, Billy and Mira to tidy up.

Harrison! Billy! Tidy up your books please.

Mira, tidy up the plates please.

8

Tidy up these groups! Can you spot the odd one in each group?

9

Lots and few

Here are lots of cars.

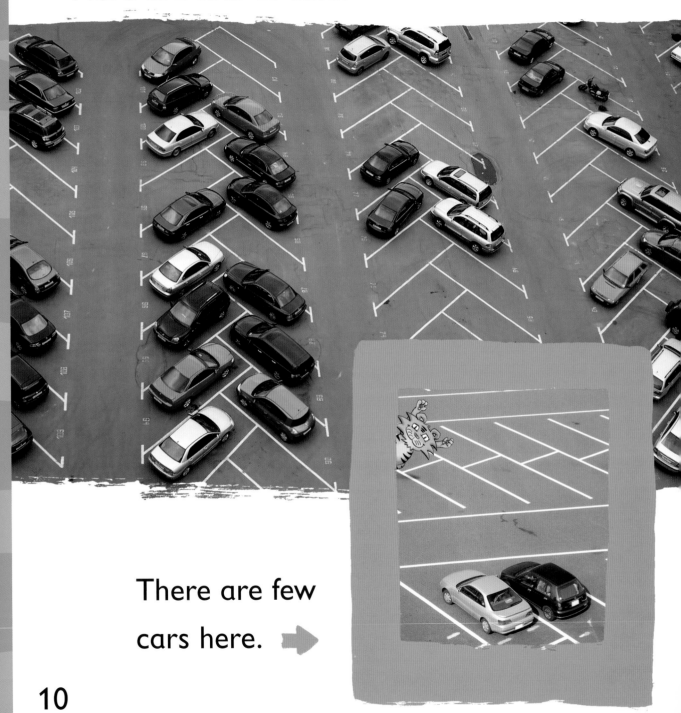

There are few cars here.

10

Here are lots of masks.

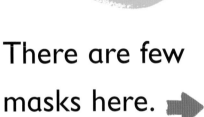

There are few
masks here. ➡

Which is your
favourite mask?

11

Sorting materials

Lola is sorting materials for recycling.

1

Felix is sorting recycled materials to make a robot.

2

He needs tubes for the arms and the legs. He covers the kitchen roll tubes in foil. They will be the arms.

Felix cuts another tube in half. He makes the two pieces into legs and covers them with foil.

Next he cuts out decorations for his robot.

Then Felix sticks on the decorations. His robot is almost finished.

He makes a robot head. Now his recycled robot is ready for action!

15

Dinner time!

Carlo and Anya are setting the table for dinner. There will be four people.

Carlo sorts out the knives and forks.

Anya sorts out the cups and plates.

How many plates does she need?

Does Anya have enough cups?

Fair sorting

Felix and Ed sort out the fruit.
Everyone has the same amount.

Lola pours out
the juice.

Everyone has the
same amount.
Now the jug is empty.

Now what has happened?
Does everyone have
the same?

Sorting shopping

Shop shelves
are sorted
into rows.

At home Lola
sorts out the
bottles and
packets.

Carlo is sorting some coins.

I have sorted the coins.

Help Anya to sort these into two groups: fruit and vegetables.

broccoli

banana

apple

orange

pear

papaya

carrot

apricot

green beans

21

Make a sorting box

1 Jenna is making a sorting box.

She gets an empty box.

2 She cuts out some strips of card.

22

3

Then Jenna glues the strips into the box.

4 Now she can use it to sort out her pens, pencils and crayons.

How could you decorate your sorting box?

23

Word picture bank

Masks – P. 11

Recycling – P. 12

Robot – P. 13, 14, 15

Shelves – P. 20

Tidy up – P. 8

Washing – P. 6, 7

First published in 2009 by Franklin Watts
338 Euston Road, London NW1 3BH

Franklin Watts Australia
Level 17/207 Kent Street, Sydney NSW 2000

Copyright © Franklin Watts 2009

Series editor: Adrian Cole
Photographer: Andy Crawford (unless otherwise credited)
Design: Sphere Design Associates
Art director: Jonathan Hair

A CIP catalogue record for this book is available
from the British Library.

ISBN: 978 0 7496 8657 4

Dewey Classification: 511

Acknowledgements:
The Publisher would like to thank Norrie Carr model agency. 'Tiger' and 'Rabbit'
puppets used with kind permission from Ravensden PLC (www.ravensden.co.uk).
Tiger Talk logo drawn by Kevin Hopgood.

Ronen/Shutterstock: 7t and 24cr (clothes). WizData Inc/Shutterstock: 11, 24tl. Norman
Pogson/Shutterstock: 10b. Nicholas Sutcliffe/Shutterstock: 3br. J. Helgason/Shutterstock: 9bl.
Andrey Khrolenok/Shutterstock: 10t. Vasiliy Koval/Shutterstock: 3bl. Edyta Pawlowska/
Shutterstock: 3tr. Dusty Cline/Shutterstock: 9t. Andriy Rovenko/Shutterstock: 20t, 24cl. Vincent
Giordano/Shutterstock: 9c (car). Nadezda/Shutterstock: 9bc. Silvano Audisio/Shutterstock:
3lc. Elena Schweitzer/Shutterstock: 9bc (brick). Stillfx/Shutterstock: 3tc. Obak/Shutterstock: 9b
(big bear). Quaxelc/Shutterstock: 9cr. Dori O'Connell/iStockphoto: 8b, 24bc.

Every attempt has been made to clear copyright. Should there be any
inadvertent omission please apply to the publisher for rectification.

Printed in China

Franklin Watts is a division
of Hachette Children's Books,
an Hachette Livre UK company.
www.hachettelivre.co.uk

There are 18 Tigers, including me, in this book. Did you find all of us?